Why Doesn't The Law Of Attraction Work?

Other books by Eliza-Jane Jackson

Creating Prosperity and Abundance (Create the life you really want)

Create Your Own Prosperity Wheel (A step-by-step guide to using the Law of Attraction to manifest the things you want)

Why Doesn't The Law Of Attraction Work?

By: Eliza-Jane Jackson

Published by: Shepherd Creative Learning

Copyright:

First published in 2014

ISBN: 978-0-9929479-0-3

Book cover designed by Cassandra Torrecillas - www.digitallybrewed.com

Copyright © Eliza-Jane Jackson 2014

Publisher's Note:

Please note: the views expressed in this e-book are those of the author.

The author has made every reasonable attempt to achieve complete accuracy of the content in this e-book prior to going to press. The publisher and the author cannot accept responsibility for any errors or omissions, however caused.

Dedication:

This e-book is dedicated to my parents and my partner, Dennis Shepherd

Dennis worked on this project with me but, unfortunately, died before we could finish and publish it. Wherever you are Dennis; here's to you!

Thank you all for believing in me even when I didn't believe in myself!

To my friends who've patiently read and reviewed this book - thank you.

Love to you all

About The Author:

Eliza-Jane has been a spiritual explorer since early childhood. She has always been inquisitive, which led to an interest in personal spiritual development at an early age.

Eliza-Jane grew up in a household where one parent had no religious or spiritual beliefs and the other had deep-seated spiritual beliefs. This provided a very interesting and thought provoking environment for a curious mind. Her parents encouraged open discussion and debate to enable their children to reach their own conclusions.

From an early age Eliza-Jane has been interested in trying to influence the direction of her life. Of course, for a long time she didn't know it had a name; the Law of Attraction.

Like most people, it took Eliza-Jane years to overcome her self-limiting beliefs. She then learnt to consciously harness the power of the Law of Attraction. This has led to a lifelong interest in the Law of Attraction, the Law of Manifestation, cosmic ordering, prosperity and abundance.

Like everyone else, Eliza-Jane's life has been littered with good fortune and setbacks. "What's different now is I embrace every experience, good or bad. I know that I will learn something from every challenge and setback. I've also learnt to be more grateful for the good things.

Today I enjoy a more peaceful and balanced life."

"Thank you Law of Attraction!"

Table of Contents

Preface:

There are hundreds (possibly even thousands) of articles and books on the subject of the Law of Attraction. So why have I chosen to write and publish this e-book? The answer is, we all have a different perspective on the success, or not, of the Law of Attraction.

Only by reading what is available can each of us make our own judgement on how effective the Law of Attraction is. This e-book is my take on the Law of Attraction. I hope by putting my views into the melting pot, I will give you another opinion to consider.

Personally, I'm a strong believer in the Law of Attraction, and have enough personal evidence to confirm that it works. I haven't always enjoyed the results of the Law of Attraction, but I do recognise and respect the power of it.

These days I try to harness the power of the Law of Attraction consciously. Spiritual enlightenment and understanding the power of the Law of Attraction have helped shape my life. Both have positively contributed to the calmer and more peaceful life I now enjoy.

Is your glass half full or half empty? Your answer ultimately affects your attitude to life. This in turn affects your life. It impacts the material goods and experiences you manifest. It even impacts your physical health and emotional wellbeing.

If your thoughts are mostly negative then you're most likely to have a pessimistic and cynical outlook on life. If your thoughts are positive you're most likely to be an optimist by nature. This statement might sound like a sweeping generalisation, but if you look at it closely you'll notice how accurate this is.

Either way, if you focus enough attention on something, good or bad, you will eventually turn it into your reality. Why not choose to focus on what you do want, rather than what you don't want? The Law of Attraction simply responds to the strength of the vibration.

The Law of Attraction offers an enticing promise to each of us. It states that each us of can attract anything we want through belief and intention. That's a big promise to make! So, are you open-minded enough to find out what the Law of Attraction can do for you?

The Law of Attraction has an important role to play in any kind of prosperity work. I have already published two other books on the subject of prosperity and abundance. The titles of these books are - Create Your Own Prosperity Wheel, and Creating Prosperity and Abundance. Both of these books can be used to help the reader use the Law of Attraction to manifest the life they want.

Thank you for choosing to read 'Why Doesn't the Law of Attraction Work?' If nothing else, I hope this book will challenge your thinking, or raise your awareness of the power of thought. I also hope you will give the Law of Attraction a chance to manifest some great things for you.

Quote: ***"Nothing is, unless our thinking makes it so"*** - Shakespeare

1. Introduction

Why doesn't the Law of Attraction work? The truth is it does work; all the time. We're all using the Law of Attraction in some way, whether we're aware of it nor not.

We're all born with the power to harness the Law of Attraction. The only person standing in the way of our success is us. There are no costs and we're not dependent on others for our success. Our success is the result of us - pure and simple!

Quote: ***"Imagination is everything. It is the preview of life's coming attractions"*** – Albert Einstein

The Law of Attraction responds to our level of intention. Sometimes we may believe it isn't working for us because it hasn't given us what we think we asked for. The reality is we said (vocalised) one thing, but our inner voice said something different. This created conflict and the Universe simply responded to the strongest vibration.

The Law of Attraction is well and working. If you've read 'The Secret' or even seen the DVD you will know the Law of Attraction does work for a lot of people. The reality is the Law of Attraction works for all of us, but 'The Secret' only focused on the success stories. Why wouldn't it; success sells more copies!

The Law of Attraction is one of the best known and most powerful of all the Universal Laws. Most people have heard of the Law of Attraction, but not everyone understands how it works. For the record, the Law of Attraction is not some 'new age' craze. It's been in existence since the creation of the Universe, and the day the 'Law of Gravity' started working.

At its simplest, the Law of Attraction is the name given to the belief that 'like attracts like'. The belief is that we all create our own realities through our thoughts and intentions. By focusing on positive or negative thoughts each of us can bring about positive or negative results.

We attract the people who come into our lives, the material goods in our homes, our professional success, and the money (or not) in our bank accounts. All of this is achieved through the strength of our vibrations (thoughts and feelings). How often have you heard people complaining about their lack of wealth, and all they attract is more of the same?

The Law of Attraction has been ridiculed by many people over the years. They dismiss the notion that our thoughts and emotions have real power in a physical world. Some sneeringly refer to the Law of Attraction as believing in a mail order catalogue in the sky. My personal view is don't reject something just because you don't understand it!

As you've chosen to read 'Why Doesn't the Law of Attraction Work?' you either believe in the Law of Attraction or are curious to know more before you decide. I hope you will keep an open mind as you read this e-book, and if nothing else will be curious to know more at the end of it.

Quote: ***"All that we are is a result of what we have thought"*** - Buddha

2. What is the Law of Attraction?

A basic definition of the Law of Attraction is 'your thoughts dictate your reality. Whatever you think about you attract into your life - whether you want it or not'.

Quantum physics shows us that at an atomic level everything in the Universe is not matter, but pure energy. Scientists have discovered that in every cell in everything, even inanimate objects, there are strings of energy, and that we all belong to the same universal system.

The Law of Attraction has been working since the day the Universe was formed. Today we know this beautiful and life transforming law as the Law of Attraction, but this name was only introduced in 1906.

The Law of Attraction is a law of nature, used by the Creator to give us the things we set our intention on. Everything in the present is the result of previous intention vibrations created by our thoughts. Think of it as the cause and effect mechanism.

The Law of Attraction is a very powerful force, which is often misunderstood. It works rather like the Law of Electricity. The Law of Electricity doesn't care whether it electrocutes us or lights up our home. The Law of attraction is the same; it doesn't care whether it creates outcomes we want or not. The Law of Attraction simply responds to the vibration.

The Law of Attraction is the magnetic power of the Universe that draws similar or compatible energies together. As everything in the Universe is energy the Law of Attraction can bring together thoughts, ideas, people, situations and circumstances. All that is needed are vibrations that match or have a strong synergy.

The Law of Attraction doesn't speak English, Italian, Arabic, Urdu or any other language known to humankind. The Law of Attraction speaks 'vibration'. It responds to our strongest vibrations i.e. the things we focus on most - good or bad.

Reflection: What are you focussing on currently?

1. Take a little time to reflect on what is capturing most of your conscious thoughts currently. Are you getting married, moving house, job hunting or dealing with a conflict situation etc?

2. Are your thoughts mostly positive or negative? Are you anticipating a positive or negative outcome?

3. Spend some time reflecting on what you've learnt and, more importantly, what you're going to do about it

Many experiences are created unwittingly as we fail to recognise the force of the Law of Attraction, and how it works. Unfortunately, we often devote more attention to the things we don't want, than the things we do want. The more passion we focus on something the faster it will happen as the Universe acts on the strength of the vibration.

Think of yourself as a magnet. This magnet has the power to draw people, material goods and experiences to you. The power of the Universe is only limited by the imagination of the energy creating the original vibration (i.e. you). This realisation can be both liberating and scary.

The Law of Attraction is sometimes referred to as 'positive thinking'. This then leads people to mention 'The Secret', which suggests The Law of Attraction is a recent phenomenon. This is not the case. As I said before, the Law of Attraction has been in existence since the beginning of time.

The Law of Attraction was given its name in 1906 by author and publisher William Walker Atkinson. He released a book called 'Thought Vibration or the Law of Attraction in the Thought World'. William Walker Atkinson introduced us to the concepts of thought, energy, vibration and manifestation in detail.

In 1910 Wallace Delois Wattles published a book, 'The Science of Getting Rich'. He explained the creative role of thought. He also further elaborated the universal role of energy as 'stuff from which others things are made'.

If you want to know more about either of these authors I suggest you type their names into your search engine.

If you want to develop a greater understanding of the science behind the Law of Attraction I recommend you read the Good Vibrations Energy Clinic article. The link to this article is http://www.goodvibesclinic.com/the-science-behind-the-law-of-attraction.

Quote: ***"Welcome to planet earth. There is nothing that you cannot be, do or have. You are a magnificent creator"*** - Abraham Hicks

3. What is the Difference Between the Law of Attraction and the Law of Manifestation?

There are many laws of natural order in the Universe. Universal laws include The Law of Manifestation (sometimes called the Law of Allowing), the Law of Accountability, the Law of Matter, and the Law of Knowledge; to name just a few.

For the purpose of this book I'm focusing on the Law of Attraction, but will briefly mention the Law of Manifestation as it's part of the Law of Attraction. The Law of Manifestation, like the Law of Attraction, is often activated without us knowing it.

The Law of Attraction is the philosophy that we are what we think. The Law of Manifestation is the action, object or happening as a result of the command. In other words, it's the process by which we apply the Law of Attraction.

The Law of Attraction process begins with a thought. This creates a vibration based on how often and how intent this thought is. The more passionate our conviction the faster the process works.

The next stage is the Law of Deliberate Creation. This sounds contradictory as we often active the Law of Deliberate Creation without being aware of it. By focusing on something we invite it in, whether we want it or not.

Belief is the most important part of the Law of Manifestation. The Law of Manifestation is the result of believing with complete certainty. So whether our belief is positive or negative the Universe will respond to the vibration. If our vibration is very strong for the things we don't want we will still manifest them.

Being rich seems to be a fairly common desire so I'll use this as an example to make my point. We start off by picturing ourselves being rich. This then creates a vibration for wealth. So far so good, but then things change.

At the same time we focus on feeling unhappy as we aren't rich yet. This creates an internal conflict. This 'lack of wealth' thought pushes our desire for wealth away as it's our current reality and is creating a stronger vibration.

Because we've created conflicting thoughts the Universe responds to the stronger vibration i.e. lack of wealth. We always draw experiences that mirror our state of mind. That's the Law of Attraction for you!

Instead of being joyous and grateful for our current wealth we notice rich people and compare ourselves against them. If we felt rich and believed that even greater wealth was ours to have it would happen.

In order for the Law of Manifestation to happen it's important to have perfect confidence that it will happen. Don't start worrying about whether this is going to happen or not, as this allows doubt to creep in. This doubt immediately reduces, or even removes, the chance of success.

Although we don't always recognise it, we put a great deal of conviction into declaring what we don't want. This is why we often attract the very things or experiences we declare we don't want. If only we worked so hard on what we do want - how different things would be.

To recap; if you want the Law of Attraction and the Law of Manifestation to work focus on the end result. Don't worry about how it's going to happen; just believe it will. The really important bit is ensuring we focus on positive outcomes, not negative ones.

We also need to know that the Law of Manifestation doesn't always give us what we want in the way we expect it. Travel through life optimistically and with an open mind. This enables us to recognise when opportunity knocks on our door. Be aware, opportunity doesn't hang around for long.

Quote: ***"Follow your bliss and the Universe will open doors where there were walls"*** - Joseph Campbell

4. How Often Does the Law of Attraction Work?

The Law of Attraction is always working. It's impossible to stop the Law of Attraction working.

As we already know, everything is energy. Energy is a constant source that can't be turned on or off at will. Therefore, this universal power is at work 24 hours a day, 365 days a year. Every second there are millions (probably more) of manifestations taking place in the Universe.

Many manifestations will be generated through conscious and intentional thought. Many more will be the result of unconscious thoughts. Furthermore, many manifestations will be unwelcome i.e. they will be things we didn't want.

Sometimes we convince ourselves that the Law of Attraction isn't working as it seems to be stubbornly failing to deliver what we've asked for. The Law of Attraction doesn't stop working, even if we stop believing. Also, it doesn't just deliver what we ask for when we ask for it; it's not quite that controllable.

With sufficient intention and complete belief the Law of Attraction will deliver what we've asked for. This doesn't always happen exactly as we've instructed. The Universe is funny like that. It will deliver the equivalent of something better, but not always what we said we wanted.

It's important to be aware and spot when things manifest for us. For example, I recently asked the Law of Attraction for a rise in income as I was struggling financially.

I expected to be given more paid work, but my income came from a totally different source; a better and more sustainable lifelong source. How great is that. On this occasion because my cosmic order was vague my expectations were exceeded.

As you begin to understand and accept the Law of Attraction you will start reducing your negative thoughts and start replacing them with positive thoughts. From this place you will begin to accept that the things in your life are the result of your initial thought process.

There are some key signs to look out for, which will confirm the Law of Attraction is at work. These are:

1. Coincidences seem to happen more often

Coincidences happen all the time. When we're consciously trying to manifest things into our life we become more aware of coincidences. These are often subtle signs that we would have previously missed.

2. Synchronicity happens more often

Synchronicity is when two unrelated events happen close together. At first the common thread may not be obvious, but on closer inspection we notice the link.

A good example of this is scientific experiments. It's common for scientists to be conducting similar experiments in different parts of the world. These experiments will be conducted by people who have no contact with each other and yet come up with the same idea at the same time.

3. We're more focused on what we want

Even if our normal modus operandi is haphazard we suddenly become more focused on what we want to achieve. We set an intention for something to happen; even if we're not aware of it. This is the unconscious deliberate Law of Deliberate Creation that I spoke about before.

The Law of Attraction may not act on this vibration quickly as our intention isn't strong, but it will be working quietly in the background. At first we may not be aware of any changes. However, gradually we will become aware that our desire is beginning to manifest.

4. Opportunities arrive at the right time

We have opportunities in our lives nearly all the time. Unfortunately, we often miss them as we seem to be sleepwalking through life.

The Law of Attraction increases our awareness and makes opportunity spotting much easier. Once we learn to make the link between opportunities and our declared intention we realise the Universe is working on our behalf.

5. We feel more in control

Being a control freak may be your natural state but we all have a hidden control freak inside us. When we accept that conscious thought can attract what we want our inner control freak rears its head.

Reflection: The things you have manifested recently

1. Spend a little time reflecting on the things you've manifested recently

2. Were these manifestations as a result of conscious or unconscious thoughts?

3. Were you please with what you manifested or not?

So in summary, the Law of Attraction is working constantly. It can't be turned on or off like a tap. If we're smart we will learn to harness the power of the Law of Attraction to manifest what we want. Otherwise, we'll simply end up with a selection of what we do and don't want. The choice is ours.

Quote: "***Whatever we plant in our subconscious mind and nourish with***

repetition and emotion will one day become a reality" - Earl Nightingale

5. Who Can Use the Law of Attraction?

Every energy source in the Universe uses the Law of Attraction. The Law of Attraction isn't restricted to humankind as a whole or even selected people. No human or inanimate object has to ask permission to use the Law of Attraction.

The world around us is constantly changing, although not every change is massive. Some changes are imperceptible initially, and we only become aware of them then the change is significant enough to be noticeable.

These changes are all the result of energy vibrations. Every manifestation starts with an intention. In the case of humans, it's a thought. The intention creates a vibration. Some vibrations are immediately strong, while others are weak.

Don't panic; not every random thought turns into a manifestation. It's the strength and consistency of intentions that create a strong enough vibration for manifestation.

Perhaps you thought about someone and the next day you heard from them. This happened due to the magnetic force of both party's thought. At or around the same time each of you thought about the other one. These energies were drawn together and manifested as a contact.

As humans we all use the Law of Attraction in our everyday lives, whether we're aware of it or not. The big secret is most people aren't aware that they're using the Law of Attraction, and may actually feel uncomfortable with the thought of manifesting without conscious thought. Not that they can stop it working of course.

The majority of us never learn to harness the power of the Law of Attraction properly. As a result we have a hit-and-miss success rate manifesting the things we claim we want. Do you genuinely believe that you can manifest what you want, or does your inner voice keep telling you it will never happen?

Two of the most common questions that people ask are: "Can I use the Law of Attraction to win the Lottery", and "why doesn't everyone use the Law of Attraction to win the Lottery?"

In theory anyone could use the Law of Attraction to win the Lottery, but it takes a little more effort than simply buying a Lottery ticket. Obviously if you don't buy the Lottery ticket then your chances of success are zero.

For many people the thought of a big win on the Lottery can be a cause of great internal conflict. We may declare that we want to win the Lottery, but our inner voice might be saying "of course it will never happen, people like me never win" etc. This internal conflict immediately gets in the way of us winning.

If we want something too badly then we end up creating a vibration that reflects need, want and lack of. This 'lack of' something creates the negative vibration that simply generates more lack. It's important to want and believe, but not to be desperate.

We assume the Law of Attraction isn't working for us because we fail to manifest the things we've declared we want. In reality, we are preventing ourselves getting what we want because our dominant thought is the opposite of our conscious statement.

The Law of Attraction and the Law of Manifestation are equally available to each of us. These laws apply to each us, in every situation and at all times. There is no exception to this rule, so being a non-believer doesn't make any difference.

Creation is constant. The Universe doesn't stop creating just because most of us are unaware of our thoughts and the consequences of these thoughts. All that happens is we attract the things our more powerful inner voice declares as it has the stronger vibration.

Once we learn to harness the power of the Law of Attraction each of us can manifest the abundant life we dream of. Our thoughts really are that powerful. Imagine how good it would feel to have some conscious control over the people, things and experiences we attract.

Instead of life being a lucky dip, we could attract what we want. Fear not, it is possible!

Quote: ***"Every single second is an opportunity to change your life, because in any moment you can change the way you feel"*** - Rhonda Byrne

6. How Does the Law of Attraction Work?

The answer to this question is not as long or complicated as you may expect. Furthermore, the Law of Attraction is not a new concept; it's been in existence since the beginning of time.

Sometimes the Law of Attraction is misinterpreted, as people assume that it should be used like a wish magnet. They simply toss their instructions out to the Universe and get on with their lives; expecting some miracle to happen.

Thoughts are powerless unless supported by intention. The Law of Attraction isn't capable of differentiating between what we want and what we don't want. It just attracts everything that has a strong enough vibration.

As humans we are energy beings and operate like magnets. Magnetic fields normally attract their polar opposite. The Law of Attraction works by using energy vibrations to attract our polar equivalents.

Whether we realise it or not, every thought has a vibration. A single thought is unlikely to create a strong vibration so don't start worrying about every thought you have.

If the thought is strong enough it sends a magnetic signal to the Universe in the form or a vibration. The Universe responds to the strength of this vibration.

The stronger the vibration the sooner we will see results. As the vibration becomes more solid it begins to manifest what we've been focusing on. This may be people, material goods or experiences. Also, the results can be things we do and don't want.

Here's an example to help make my point: If you focus on getting married eventually the Universe will give you the wedding you wanted. This doesn't mean you will marry the perfect partner, or the relationship will survive the test of time.

You set the intention of getting married, and this happened. If you didn't also make the intention a long and happy marriage with the right person you may not get this part. It's important to understand that the Universe is very literal. The Universe acts on our vibration, not our oral instructions.

Reflection: Something I consciously manifested

1. Spend a little time reflecting on something you manifested through conscious thought. For example, this might be your wedding, new job, new home etc

2. Did you get exactly what you asked for?

3. Was this the same as you wanted it to be? For example - a friend of mine asked for a new car. She got the right car, colour and price, but she didn't ask for problem free motoring. Her new car has already been hit and scraped by four other drivers.

Here's another example: If you keep focusing on living in your dream home eventually this will become your reality. Of course, your vision of a dream home may change over time so the dream home you end up living in may be very different from the one your initially wanted.

Lack of wealth is something lots of people focus on. If we constantly focus on lack of wealth we will simply attract more of the same. Far from getting out of poverty we draw more poverty to ourselves. This is because lack and scarcity are our dominant thoughts and so create the strongest vibration.

It's our choice whether we want to focus on positive or negative outcomes. We alone are the controller of our thoughts. Therefore, we control how the Law of Attraction works for each of us. The more in-tune on we are the more control we will have over the result.

Each of us can manifest the things we truly want, but so often we feel disappointed when we don't get exactly what we claimed we wanted. Apply the rules properly and we can harness the power of the Law of Attraction to deliver exactly what we want.

The rules of engagement are very straightforward:

1. We need to be very clear about what we want and have a strong enough desire for it. We need to be able to describe our desired outcome, experience or item in detail

2. We need to have the motivation and commitment to do what's necessary to achieve our goal e.g. act on the opportunities when they appear

3. We need to be able to persistently visualise what we want to manifest. This requires a degree of self-discipline as we tend to drift off-course

4. We need to be open to spotting opportunities, and willing to accept the opportunities presented to us. If we hesitate too long, the opportunity often disappears

5. We need to be willing to act when required. It's no good resting on our laurels and expecting the Universe to put in all the effort

6. We need to appreciate and enjoy it when we get it (whatever 'it' is); not simply start reaching out for something new

The Law of Attraction is not a 'get rich quick scheme'. It requires some effort, belief and visualisation, as well as a willingness to take action. In short, we have to take responsibility for making the Law of Attraction work for us. The reward for our efforts can be spectacular.

Let's use winning the Lottery as an example again. Imagine you've declared that you want to win the Lottery. It's clearly achievable as lots of people do it.

Are you willing to buy a Lottery ticket every week until you win? Or, will you buy a single ticket and give up when it doesn't give you an instant result? Alternatively, will you just buy a Lottery ticket when you remember to do it?

Next, there's more than one Lottery draw each week, so exactly which Lottery draw are you interested in?

Do you have a specific sum in mind, or will you be content with any prize? When people talk about winning the Lottery they are generally talking about being the main prize winner. In order to achieve this you need to focus on being the main prize winner.

Can you visualise yourself winning and clearly see how you will spend your winnings?

How motivated are you really? Are you willing to maintain the strength of the vibration until you achieve your goal? Or, will your intention weaken when you don't get an instant result?

I have a friend who regularly tells me that she's going to win the Lottery. Sure enough she does win regularly. She usually wins £5 or £25, and then feels terribly disappointed as she didn't get what she wanted.

She consistently fails to play her part to bring about her desired outcome. The Universe gives her what she asks for - a Lottery win. Until she learns to harness the Law of Attraction her chances of winning the jackpot are slim.

Quote: ***"Our subconscious minds have no sense of humour, play no jokes and cannot tell the difference between reality and an imagined thought or image. What we continually think about will eventually manifest in our lives"*** - Robert Collier

7. Some Examples of the Law of Attraction Working

It's sometimes difficult for us to accept something without proof. Obviously I could provide hundreds of examples of the success of the Law of Attraction. I'm just going to suggest a few common examples I hope you can relate to.

Perhaps you spent a large part of your adult life looking for that 'special' relationship. You may have convinced yourself it wasn't going happen. It's those conflicting messages again - you want the relationship, but don't believe it will happen.

Until your intention (vibration) changed Mr or Miss Right didn't appear in your life. Whether you're aware of it or not, your deep-seated beliefs did change. This shift in energy enabled you to attract that special person into your life.

As I've previously stated, wealth is a common theme when people talk about the Law of Attraction. However, not everyone wants to win vast sums of money on the Lottery. Sometimes we're seeking a loan or would like a small amount of money for a specific purpose.

Let's deal with the loan first. You put a thought (intention) out to the Universe that you wanted a loan. Another energy source had some money to invest. The Universe then recognised the synergy and brought the two energies together. Think of this as magnetic forces in action.

Alternatively, imagine that you needed a specific sum of money to pay for some work to be done. You may not have given you the cash, but someone may have offered to do the job free of charge.

You manifested what you wanted, just not in the way you expected. Your stronger vibration was what the funds were required for, rather than the actual money. It's that opportunity spotting I mentioned in chapter six.

Henry Ford is a classic example of the Law of Attraction working. It took quite some time for his engineers to create his vision; a car for the masses.

Many of us would have given up; believing the goal was too difficult to achieve. Henry Ford didn't give up; he stayed focused on his goal and so strengthened the vibration. Eventually his dream, the Model T Ford was created. This wouldn't have happened if he hadn't believed and stayed focused.

Here's an example of the Law of Attraction working in response to a negative intention. Perhaps your manager is giving you a hard time at work, or worse still, you're the victim of workplace bullying.

Your initial thought is probably I would never wish that on myself. Unfortunately, the reality is that's exactly what you've done. You allowed your negative thoughts to create a vibration that was strong enough to attract an energy to fulfil your request.

Secondly, no matter how unpalatable the thought, you are getting something from this experience. Many of us actually get some perverse pleasure from being a victim; although we would never admit this to anyone.

John Assaraf's story is another example of the success of the Law of Attraction, and can easily be verified. If you don't already know John Assaraf's story and want to know more type his name into a search engine. You will find lots of information available.

John Assaraf puts his success down to forming a positive mental attitude, thinking positively, nurturing positive thoughts and diminishing negative thoughts. Added to this, he focused on his desire to amplify the vibration, and persistently believed in the eventual outcome.

If we don't like the things we're manifesting we need to take control and start creating positive vibrations. If John Assaraf's attitude seems like too much effort then you haven't found the thing that motivates you sufficiently yet. If we create a strong enough vibration we can attract it.

Every part of our life experience is the Law of Attraction's response to our previous intentions i.e. cause and effect. Changing our thinking changes the vibrations, which in turn changes the results eventually. Don't expect instant results though.

Everything we experience from prosperity to poverty, and happiness to grief, is the result of earlier intentions. By learning to harness the power of the Law of Attraction we can have far greater control over our lives.

We all experience grief, setbacks and unpleasant situations. It's part of our human existence to experience some negative situations. However, we choose whether to go through life experiencing problem after problem, or viewing setbacks as opportunities to learn something. This positive mental attitude lessens the negative impact unpleasant experiences.

Quote: ***"A man is but the product of his thoughts. What he thinks he becomes"*** - Gandhi

8. What Can I Use the Law of Attraction For?

Obviously we can harness the Law of Attraction to attract material goods. We can also use the Law of Attraction to bring people into our lives. Some use it for experiences, health, contentment, and emotional wellbeing.

The Law of Attraction is only limited by our imagination. If we're able to believe the sky's the limit we can attract anything we wish.

If we choose to, we can harness the Law of Attraction for every aspect of our lives. The most common uses of the Law of Attraction are:

1. Money and financial prosperity
2. Jobs and careers
3. Finding that 'special' person/relationship
4. Strengthening an existing relationship
5. Finding a new home
6. Having a family, or adding to the family
7. Good physical health
8. Emotional and spiritual wellbeing
9. Achieving personal goals
10. A dream lifestyle

If our beliefs are limited then this will be reflected in the results we achieve. When we truly believe that anything is possible the world is our oyster.

It's important to remember one person's idea of wealth could be someone else's idea of poverty. That's why it's so important to be clear and specific about what you truly want, as well as believing it's possible.

The Law of Attraction can successfully play a part in the business world too; even if the marketplace appears chaotic. It's far too easy to buy into the concept that 'the economy is in a terrible state' and every business is therefore doomed. The media certainly plays its part in maintaining this hype.

It's important not to get caught up in this frenzy, and to remember that not every business is failing. Far from it! People are still prospering. Some businesses are still thriving and many entrepreneurs are starting new businesses. These are the people who have chosen prosperity over poverty.

It's now common for motivational speakers and business coaches to promote the Law of Attraction as a mechanism for business success.

Whether you want to use the Law of Attraction for personal or business use, the process is the same. There are three basic elements to the Law of Attraction. These are:

1. The philosophy of the Law of Attraction

2. The Law of Deliberate Creation

3. The Law of Manifestation, sometimes known as 'Allowing'

If you want to use the Law of Attraction for a new business, think about the type of business and product/service offering. For an existing business focus on the customers/clients you want. Alternatively, visualise the lifestyle being an entrepreneur will bring you.

Be careful not to focus on problem clients or any financial difficulties as this will just create more of the same.

If you really want to see what the Law of Attraction can be used for don't allow your logical and conscious mind to set limited parameters. Think differently i.e. 'think outside the box' and get bigger and better results.

In order to manifest the things you've never had before you need to first think about things you've never dared to dream of before. Make these big, bright and larger than life size thoughts your new intention. Who knows where your imagination may take you in future.

Exercise: My number one goal

1. Think of a single thing you would really like to have in your life or your business

2. Imagine your goal in as much detail as possible

3. See yourself enjoying every aspect of tis; as if you've already got it

You can either start with small goals and build up to something big, or start with the massive goal principle. The choice is yours.

If you want to know more about the massive goal principle I suggest you visit the Stretch Development Limited website. The website address is - http://www.stretchdevelopment.com.

Quote: ***"Take the first step in faith. You don't have to see the whole staircase. Just take the first step"*** - Dr Martin Luther King Jr.

9. Money and the Law of Attraction

Money is one of the first things people think about when you mention the Law of Attraction. Therefore, I've given money its own chapter; even though the same principles apply to manifesting money or anything else.

Money is essential for living, but we also need to adopt a healthy attitude to money beyond this. Of course, we all use money to buy the basic necessities of life. We also use money to buy the 'little', or not so little, extras that make our lives easier and more fun.

I've already explained that everything is energy and that all energy belongs to the same universal system. Each type of energy has its own vibration. Money is an energy that has its own vibration too.

Money can be your friend or foe. If you have a positive and healthy attitude to money you make it possible for money to flow to you and through you effortlessly. Very rich people seem to continually get richer, while the poor often appear to get poorer. This is partly due to their attitude to money.

Very rich people have a healthy attitude to money. They are happy to spend or invest their wealth. Although this benefits their life in some way; often material goods, it also benefits others too. For instance, if a very rich person buys your products or services your wealth increases too. This in turn creates a healthy wealth cycle.

If you have a negative attitude to money this vibration will create an energy block. If you constantly focus on how little money you have you'll attract more of the same - a lack of perceived wealth.

Quote: ***"If you're thinking of debt that's what you're going to attract"*** - Bob Proctor

If you have wealth but refuse to it then you create an energy blockage. Energy blockages don't help anyone. Money, like any other energy, needs to keep flowing.

If you want to test your attitude to money, ask yourself the following questions. Be sure to answer the questions truthfully:

1. Do you think or feel you don't deserve to be wealthy?

2. Do you believe that people like you never get rich?

3. As a child were you taught that you have to work hard to have money?

4. As a child were you constantly told that 'money doesn't grow on trees'?

5. Do you worry about having sufficient money to pay your bills?

6. Do you constantly worry about where 'the money' is going to come from?

7. Do you feel envious or resentful when you meet wealthy people?

If your answers to these questions are 'yes' you have an unhealthy attitude to money. Unless you choose to change this vibration you will continually experience a lack of financial prosperity.

It doesn't matter what you were told about money as child, that's history. You have a choice; either stick with your old beliefs or adopt a more positive vibration regarding money and see what happens.

If you keep telling yourself you have insufficient money; trust me, that's exactly what you'll keep manifesting. Until this becomes too painful to bear any longer you will continue to struggle financially.

I'm not suggesting that adopting a positive and healthy attitude to money will make you a millionaire. However, if you want money to form a beneficial part of your life it's definitely worth developing a positive money vibration.

Developing a positive attitude to money may take time and effort. Old habits can be hard, but not impossible, to break. The more comfortable you feel receiving and giving money the easier it will be to attract money into your life.

It's important to achieve a balance where you feel comfortable receiving and spending or giving money. If you receive money you must be willing to spend or share your wealth with others. This keeps the wealth flowing. This is not an exact science, but you should be willing to spend or share a good percentage of what you receive.

If you attract wealth, but are unwilling to allow others to benefit too then you effectively create a dam. Simply put; stopping other people benefiting from money will create stagnation or even poverty.

If you're having difficulty developing a positive attitude to money the following affirmations may help:

1. I have sufficient money to pay my bills

2. I have enough money for all my needs and the things that are important to me

3. I will always have the money to pay for what I need

4. I will always have spare funds to pay for the extras I want in my life

5. My income is constantly increasing and I prosper wherever I turn

6. I have plenty of money. It comes to me easily and effortlessly

7. Money and success come to me easily

If you're going to use affirmations, it's important to say and believe the words. Simply saying these affirmations once and forgetting about them won't get the desired result. You need to repeat these affirmations daily until they become feel like your reality.

Always treat your money with respect. Be grateful for the money you have, and never take it for granted. Look at the notes and coins in your wallet/purse. Get to know the faces on your bank notes, and wonder about the journey your money has already been on.

Finally, bless the money and wish it well on its onward journey. There's enough money in the world for all of us if we just learn to share a little.

Quote: ***"Be thankful for what you have, you'll end up having more. If you concentrate on what you don't have, you will never have enough"*** - Oprah Winfrey

10. How Do I Get Started?

In order to start attracting the people, materials goods and experiences we want we need to understand how the Law of Attraction works. If you've read the previous chapters you will already have a good idea of how the Law of Attraction works.

As a gentle reminder; we manifest the things that we focus on. Imagine the Universe as being dyslexic. It can't differentiate between want and don't want so it responds to the strongest vibration.

Reflection: My attitude to the Law of Attraction

1. Before we go any further, get to know yourself a little better. In particular, hear what your inner voice is telling you

2. Do you believe the Law of Attraction can work for you? Does your inner voice regularly tell you that you can't have or can't achieve something?

3. If your inner voice is holding you back, are you willing to overcome this obstacle?

4. Finally, do you have the commitment to stay focused and believe 100% until you achieve your goals?

If our intention is strong enough it will generate a vibration. As this vibration becomes more solid it begins the process of manifestation. There is no fixed timescale from thought to manifestation.

The speed of delivery is partly due to the strength of the vibration. It's also down to the will of the Universe. The Universe delivers what we ask for when the time is right, which isn't always when we want it.

We don't always like hearing that our thoughts and feelings create our experiences, especially if the results are unwelcome. The good news is once you understand the Law of Attraction you can harness its power. This will enable you to start attracting the things you truly want.

It's common knowledge that the wealthy and poor act and think differently. Do you believe that Bill Gates used to walk around saying "I'm broke; I'll never have any money". Of course not! He may not have anticipated his level of success but I'm sure he believed in his product. We all know how successful Microsoft is.

Wealthy people believe they will always have money, and so are always thinking of innovative ways to create more. Wealthy people understand that they have a part to play in creating their wealth. I'm not suggesting they all believe in the Law of Attraction though.

Obviously developing this mindset doesn't automatically guarantee unlimited wealth, but it will certainly increase our chances. Whatever the outcome we will have more than we started with.

Money may not be everyone's aspiration but the same principles apply to all goals and desires. Harnessing the Law of Attraction is a journey not a destination so be kind and gentle with yourself. Recognise and reward every success. This positive attitude will help create more prosperity and abundance.

It's not difficult to successfully use the Law of Attraction, but like any skill it does take time, effort and practice to perfect. Once you've harnessed the Law of Attraction you could achieve amazing results.

There are lots of ways to harness the Law of Attraction. Cosmic ordering and prosperity wheels (vision boards) are two common methods of using the Law of Attraction. These are covered in my books - 'Creating Prosperity and Abundance (Create the life you really want)' and 'Create Your Own Prosperity Wheel'.

If you've never tried harnessing the Law of Attraction before the following might help to get you started:

Exercise: The things I want and the things I don't want

It's important to understand whether your natural mindset is glass half full or glass half empty. Armed with this information you can take the appropriate action to harness the Law of Attraction.

Step 1: Draw two columns on a sheet of paper. Label column one 'The things I want' and label column two 'The things I don't want'. Now work on your lists.

Note: step one may take hours, days or weeks to complete. There's no need to rush; the Law of Attraction isn't going anywhere.

Step 2: On reflection, which list was easier to create? If your 'don't want' list is longer or was easier to create it's important to work on your thinking. Otherwise, you're likely to end up with the things you don't want to manifest.

Step 3: So far so good. Now you understand why you have previously attracted the things you do and don't want. Use this new knowledge to harness the Law of Attraction to attract the people, material goods and experiences you want in future.

You can revisit this exercise as often as you like. Over time our 'do and don't wants' change so it's a good idea to tune into yourself periodically.

Note: Don't consult anyone when you do this exercise. Rely on your intuition for the answers, rather than being persuaded by others. This is your 'do and don't want' list, not someone else's.

Quote: "***The Universe never asked you to struggle. It is simply answering your mood***"
- Abraham Hicks

Meditation can have benefits in all aspects of our lives, but it definitely has a role to play in the Law of Attraction. Mediation can help to remove the self-limiting beliefs that hold us back. The main philosophy of the Law of Attraction is seeing ourselves as already in possession of the things we want.

The first step is to be able to successfully meditate. Once you've mastered the art of meditation, move onto visualisation. This is the element that works with the Law of Manifestation.

Exercise: Visualisation

1. Close your eyes and begin with some deep breathing

2. Breathe in deeply through your nose, holding your breath to a count of four and then exhaling slowly through your mouth. Repeat this until you feel relaxed

3. When you feel completely relaxed you're ready to begin your visualisation

4. Ask yourself what you want to manifest in your life. This exercise works best if you focus on just one goal per visualisation. If you turn it into a lengthy shopping list you will find it harder

to create clear images and feelings of everything you want

5. Say you want a new car - fix your mind on everything about the car, colour, make, model, engine size, features etc. See yourself driving it and see it parked on your driveway. Imagine the car in as much detail as you possibly can. Try to smell the newness of the car too, and feel the pleasure it gives you

6. Fix your mindset to believe this is really going to manifest for you. Try not to fix a timescale as the Universe prefers to deliver things in its timescale rather than ours

7. Revisit your visualisation regularly, preferably daily, until you manifest your goal

8. Once you've got what you asked for, remember to thank the Universe and say, feel and think the pleasure you're getting from this item or experience

Now we've explored how to get started with the Law of Attraction, it's time to make it a way of life. In the next chapter I have provided more information about the process of ask, believe and receive.

Quote: ***"If you can dream it, you can do it"*** - Walt Disney

11. Ask, Believe and Receive

There are just three steps to successfully harnessing the Law of Attraction. These three steps are ask, believe and receive. In order to guarantee success we need to apply the correct rules to each step of the process.

1. Ask:

It sounds so simple doesn't it - just ask for what you want and hey presto the magic happens. If it was that simple every random thought we have, and every stated desire would result in manifestation. Sorry, it takes a little more effort than that.

We can all harness the Law of Attraction and the Law of Manifestation to attract the things we truly want. There's no limit to what we can ask for. In theory each of us could attract absolutely anything we want. Our requests are only limited by our imagination.

When asked "what do you truly want in your life?" most of us struggle to clearly define our desired outcomes. However, at the drop of a hat we can list all the things we don't want.

Most of us would agree that we would welcome more money. A frequently expressed desire is "I want to win the Lottery". This isn't sufficiently clear to bring about the exact success you're seeking.

Why? The answer is you haven't created a clear vibration of your desire to enable to Universe to give you exactly what you want. The questions that immediately spring to mind are: How much do you want to win, do you have a timescale in mind for your success, and what steps are you willing to take to make it possible?

In order to guarantee success we have to be very clear and specific about what we want to attract. For example, most people want more money, but ask yourself how you want to get this new wealth. Do you want to win money, win new clients who will contribute to your business success, get a promotion at work etc? The possibilities are endless.

If we can't clearly define our goals it's totally unreasonable to expect the Universe to deliver what we want. It's important to remember, each of us has a role to play in our own success. The clearer and stronger the vibration our greater the chances of success.

We should never ask the Universe for things we don't truly want. Also don't ask for anything that will harm someone else in the process of delivering what you want. A very common example is asking for someone who is already in a relationship with someone else.

Once we've decided what we truly want we need to express it in a way the Universe can understand. Miscommunication is a common human trait. How often have you thought you made your point clearly, only for the other person to receive a different message?

Ask; the stronger the vibration the greater our chances of success. Be very clear and focused on what you want. Don't fall into the age old habit of telling the Universe all the things you don't want. Remember the only language the Universe understands is vibration, so make your request is clear and strong.

2. Believe:

Belief really is key to the success of the Law of Attraction; it's the most important part of the philosophy. Many of us struggle with this part of the Law of Attraction as 'believing' often requires us to overcome some deep-seated thinking.

Do you believe in coincidences? If not, you're already in conflict with the Law of Attraction. This internal conflict is highly likely to affect your success rate.

Alternatively, do you start out with a strong belief and then take your eye off the ball? It's important to revisit your cosmic order regularly to keep the vibration strong. A good way to do this is to write your cosmic order down and read what you've written regularly. Each time you read your cosmic order see, think and feel yourself living the experience/outcome.

Some like to create a prosperity wheel (vision board). If so, place it somewhere you will see it regularly. Each time you look at it see, think and feel yourself enjoying your stated desire. The more powerful your belief the sooner you'll manifest what you want.

Although it's important for us to believe in the outcome, it's also important that we're relaxed and not desperate for our desired outcome. Desperation creates conflicting emotions, which severely hampers the chances of success.

I can't stipulate the point about belief strongly enough. In order to successfully attract the things we want we need to consistently believe that it will happen. The easiest way to do this is by convincing ourselves that it's already ours. This is why prosperity teachers often tell us to imagine that we already have what we're asking for.

We need to believe 100%, not just 99%. Push all doubts away, as the idea of failure can mess up the delivery of what you want. Just keep affirming until your desire becomes your reality.

Reflection: What stops me believing?

Spend a little time understanding what stops you believing that you will be successful in manifesting what you want.

Exercise: Affirmations to overcome my self-limiting beliefs

Self-limiting beliefs are a major hindrance. They can seriously hamper our ability to harness the Law of Attraction.

1. Write some affirmations that will help you to overcome your self-limiting belies. For example - prosperity surrounds me, prosperity fills me, and prosperity flows to me and through me

2. Read and absorb your affirmations each day until you notice a shift in your attitude

3. Receive:

This is when we start to reap the rewards of our previous thought vibrations. If we're attracting the things we want in our life this phase is very exciting. If we're attracting the things we don't want we feel frustrated and ungrateful rather than joyous.

Manifesting is no different to any other skill we have. It needs to be learnt and practised in order to be perfected. The good news is all of us are born with the inner power to use the Law of Attraction.

The most successful Law of Attraction users have trained their minds to focus on their desires. They have perfected the art to such a degree that they probably don't always realise they're doing it.

It's important that we become an active player in achieving our goals; not stand on the side-lines as a spectator. Opportunities are sometime presented to us from unexpected sources or in unexpected ways. It's important that we keep an open mind and become aware when opportunities present themselves to us. Don't hesitate, grab opportunities with both hands.

If you've ever seen the film 'Evan Almighty' you may remember Morgan Freeman's quote about happiness. If not, this is what he said "when you ask for happiness, do you think God sends someone named happiness?" All he's saying is be observant enough to recognise it when you get what you asked for.

The essence at the heart of the Law of Attraction is positivity.

Visualisation can be a useful tool in harnessing the Law of Attraction. Some like to start with a meditation, while others prefer to go straight to the visualisation. It's a matter of personal choice. Either way visualisation is a very powerful tool.

The process of visualisation requires us to define our goals clearly. The next stage is to visualise (see and feel) our new life as if we've already achieved our goals. This can be a helpful tool for anyone who struggles with the 'believe' part of ask, believe and receive.

Exercise: Visualisation and the Law of Attraction

1. Think of one thing you would like to attract into your life. For example, do you want a new car, a dog, a new job, Mr or Miss Right, your dream home etc? The possibilities are endless

2. Describe your goal. Make you description as detailed as possible. Think details, details, details. Imagine for a moment that you want a new car. Think about the make and model, colour, engine size and additional features. Does it have to be a brand new car, or a second-hand car?

Include every detail you possibly can. Visualise it and see yourself enjoying what you've attracted

3. It's really important that you totally believe that you're going to get what you're seeking. If you want to be sure of success, don't allow doubt to creep in.

The Universe will deliver your heart's desire to you when the time is right. This might not be exactly when you want it, but it will come at the right time. Furthermore, you may not get what you want in the way you're anticipating it.

A question that's often asked is "can we leave it all to the Universe?" The answer is no' the Universe has its part to play but so do each of us.

We have two roles to play in the Law of Attraction. Our first role is to clearly define our intentions and desires. We need to be very strong and clear about what we want in order to create the right vibration. Our second role is to believe (100%) in the outcome.

The Universe will present us with opportunities but it's our choice to take them or not. Ideally we shouldn't be too prescriptive about when or how the Universe should deliver our hearts desires. Equally, it's not good just sitting back and expecting everything to land in our laps.

Quote: ***"I will see it when I believe it"*** - Wayne Dyer

12. Gratitude and the Law of Attraction

One of the quickest ways to create a more prosperous and harmonious life is to start focusing on gratitude. Gratitude is a spiritual (not religious) practice of faith and expectation in actions. It's an important part of the Law of Attraction and the Law of Manifestation.

Gratitude is a very high vibrational energy, which expands the good in our life. In fact, gratitude is one of the most powerful energies in the Universe as it offers so many benefits.

How can such a simple technique create such impressive change? Basically, the more gratitude and thanks we express the more wellbeing we attract into our life. Gratitude is about more than just saying thank you. It's about feeling and showing gratitude for what we have.

In case you're reading this and thinking my life is awful, what have I got to be grateful for? Stop! We all have something to be thankful for. Even if you're just alive, that deserves appreciation. Think of the alternative!

Reflection: My personal gratitude list

Before we go any further you might like to spend a little time reflecting on all the things you're grateful for. This could be your health, the people in your life, material goods, and experiences. The list is endless

1. Write a list of all the things you're grateful for in your life currently

2. Review your list regularly, as it's easy to slip into the mindset of 'what have I got to be grateful for?'

Much of our prosperity is the result of gratitude. For some, prosperity means money and material goods. For others it will be spiritual and emotional wellbeing. True prosperity comes from feeling gratitude in all aspects of our lives.

It's important to understand that prosperity is not an external state; it's something we experience in our mind and thoughts. Gratitude means we can experience prosperity at any level of income, at any time in our life.

It's a fundamental Law of the Universe that what we focus on grows (whether good or bad). This is why it's so important to **stop** focusing on the things you don't want in your life.

Quote: "*Develop and attitude of gratitude and give thanks for everything that happens to you. Knowing that every step forward is a step towards achieving something bigger and better than your current situation*" - Brian Tracy

The more effort we make to see the benefits in every situation the more benefits we will notice. The more benefits we notice the more good things and experience we will attract. As I've already said, the Law of Attraction works on the principle of like attracts like.

Here are four examples of like attracting like for you to consider:

1. The more positive you are the more positive people you will attract into your life

2. The more prosperous you think you are the more prosperous you'll become

3. The more grateful you are the more you will attract to be grateful for

4. The more you appreciate your health the better your health will be

This list is endless, but hopefully you get the idea.

Adopting an attitude of gratitude may not be a magic solution to all our problems. However, it can help each of us to embrace a more peaceful and satisfied state of mind. This in itself is a priceless gift.

If we spend our time brooding about how awful life is the chances are we will miss the opportunities when they come along. Gratitude creates a vibration that can attract an endless supply of goodness, wealth, prosperity and abundance.

We should all get into the habit of giving thanks on a daily basis. Here's a short gratitude exercise to get you started:

Exercise: Daily Gratitude

1. Each day write down five things that you're grateful for on that day. Typical examples may be - you wake to the sun streaming through your window, spending time with your family etc. The options are endless

2. It's important to do this short exercise every day until gratitude becomes a natural mindset for you

A word of caution: don't fake it; gratitude must be genuine. If you create fake gratitude the vibration won't be strong and the results won't be the prosperity you're seeking.

Here are two further gratitude exercises you might like to try:

Exercise: Take a Gratitude Walk

1. Take a short walk each day, or as often as you possibly can

2. Look around you and take in all the natural wonders your see (plants, birds, flowers, scenery, the sky, breeze etc)

3. Give gratitude for what you see and its purpose in life. Also give thanks for your amazing body and eyes. Your body has made

this walk possible, and your eyes enable you to see and appreciate everything

4. At the end of your walk notice how refreshed you feel

Exercise: Daily Affirmations

If you're new to gratitude or just struggle to feel grateful, try some of these daily affirmations:

1. I'm grateful for all the business opportunities and customers that are drawn to me

2. Thank you for my physical health and emotional wellbeing

3. Thank you for the love, peace and happiness that I have

4. I'm grateful for my family and friends

5. I'm grateful for all the money I have and, and I see it multiply easily and effortlessly

6. I'm grateful for my lovely, safe home

7. Thank you for the food and warmth I have

8. I'm grateful to be alive

9. Thank you for giving me success in my job

10. I'm grateful for feeling happy in my own skin

You don't need to use these affirmations; you may prefer to create your own.

Cultivating gratitude has changed the lives of millions. I'm just one of them. Giving thanks is so much healthier than constantly thinking 'woe is me'.

Express gratitude for every aspect of your life. This includes your talents and abilities, sense of humour, achievements and qualities etc.

Remember our external reality mirrors our internal beliefs. By changing our inner thinking we can change our external reality.

Personally, I'm grateful that you've chose to read my e-book. Thank you!

Quote: ***"When our minds are resonating with gratitude the gate is fully opened to the flow of prosperity"*** - Dr Darryl Pokea

13. Why Isn't the Law of Attraction Working For Me?

In reality, the Law of Attraction is working for each of us, all the time. It might not be delivering what we've said we want to attract, but that's down to our thoughts (vibrations).

Quote: *"A person is what he/she thinks about all day long"* - Ralph Waldo Emerson

The Law of Attraction responds to the strongest vibration. If we declare that we want to win the Lottery but our inner voice says it will never happen we create internal conflict

Our inner voice is creating a lack of belief. This lack of belief added to want (current lack of) creates the stronger vibration. The internal conflict we've created reduces our removes our chances of success.

A question for you - "do you surround yourself with negative people?" If so, remove yourself from their clutches. Negative people and negative mind-sets seriously hamper the Law of Attraction.

If you're currently attracting the things you don't want know that the Law of Attraction is working. It's simply giving you what you're focusing on. Now you know this, focus on what you do want.

Changing our mindset can be a slow and tedious process; after all it's probably taken a long time to get to this point. We may need to work on our beliefs about money, love, health and wellbeing, material goods and experiences.

The key to success is to focus with a never wavering determination. In short, we need to devote as much time, effort and energy to positive thoughts as we've spent on negativity in the past.

Reflection: My attitude

1. Spend a little time reflecting on your attitude to money, love, what other people have and how you feel about yourself

2. This soul searching might be painful but it's a positive step towards a better life.

Do you spend a lot of time being cynical, constantly criticising others and making derisory comments about rich people? Do you say things like "rich people are greedy" or "rich people get their wealth at the expense of others?" If so, stop right now. While you maintain this negative attitude the Law of Attraction will find it difficult to bring good things to you.

Quote: *"Givers get given to"* - Russell Simmons

The thoughts we have about others reflects our deep-rooted thoughts about ourselves. It's a clear indication that we have some self-esteem issues to tackle. Until resolved we won't feel the positive effects of the Law of Attraction.

How we feel about ourselves determines what we expect from life. Our expectations then determine what we attract. Remember, like attracts like! The Law of Attraction can be our friend or foe; the choice is ours.

Exercise: Self-worth inventory

If you have self-esteem issues you may feel uncomfortable valuing all the things that make you the person you are. If so, try the self-worth inventory exercise:

1. Imagine looking at yourself as your friends and family see you. This removes the ego from the situation, and makes it easier to be objective

2. Describe the person you see. Imagine you're describing a friend to someone who has never met you

3. Your description can be physical characteristics, personality, talents, skills and achievements or anything else you like

4. Review this list regularly until you genuinely like the person you are

Learning to be kind to ourselves is a massive step in changing our situation. Genuinely wanting to be happy is a good place to start this amazing journey. As our self-worth increases so does our vibration. This is turn attracts bigger and better things into our lives.

It's important to say that some people will never break their negative thoughts and habits. Although a sad realisation, we have to accept that this is their choice. We can't force our will on others, no matter how well intentioned.

If you're serious about harnessing the Law of Attraction to attract the things you want start by learning to like, value and appreciate you. No, this is not an ego trip! This is exactly what I mean about negativity. Look at your self-worth inventory again.

Like everyone else I've subconsciously manifested things and experiences in my life. Many have been great but some experiences have been both painful and very unwelcome. Eventually I felt sufficient pain to make me change my attitude. This couldn't happen until my inner voice was ready to accept change.

Once I mastered the Law of Attraction I started to receive the things and experiences I truly wanted. Of course, occasionally I slip back into my old habits, but not for long.

If the Law of Attraction isn't manifesting what your conscious mind says it wants then start working on your subconscious. The sooner you start the sooner you'll benefit from great things the Law of Attraction has to offer.

Quote: ***"To accomplish great things we must not only act, but also dream; not only plan but also believe"*** - Anatole France

14. The Law of Attraction and the Rest of the World

People often want to know how we can use the Law of Attraction to help others. In short, we can't. Each of us can only use the Law of Attraction for our own wants and desires. Focus on what you want and allow everyone else in the world to do the same.

Although we think we know what others want in reality we don't. We can't get inside other people's heads and see what makes them genuinely happy. It's important to remember that not everyone wants what we want. Therefore, we should stop trying to force our will on others as no-one gains from this.

Reflection: Examples of trying to force my will on others

1. Spend a little time reflecting on occasions when you have tried to force your will on others. For example, are you one of those people who wants to stop world poverty and campaigns for this?

2. Do you have resentful thoughts about the wealth or luxury lifestyle of people you know?

The good news is the Universe has more than enough to go round. Prosperity and abundance means something different to each of us; we all want different things. Understanding this often helps us to feel less guilty when we appear to have more than others.

Some of us are seeking material goods and financial wealth. Others will be interested in emotional and spiritual wellbeing, rather than material goods. In both cases we will have limited interest in each other's desires. As long as we can all accept each other's differences we can create harmony.

On the reverse of this; it's human nature to want success for ourselves but not have the same wish for others. Instead we focus on resenting what others have. This is partly why we have disharmony in the world.

If everyone in the world wanted world peace it would happen due to the strength of the vibration. Until enough people want world peace humankind will never experience this or world prosperity and abundance.

As humanity becomes more enlightened so the desire for world peace increases. Slowly we will start to see the effects of this manifest and spread. You may already have noticed a growing movement towards enlightenment.

If we really want to make a difference we should start by moving forward with our own positive thoughts. This includes the things we want to manifest in our life, and wishing success for others. The more people who do this, the stronger the vibration we will create.

A colleague of mine wants to see an end to world poverty. She's constantly saying it's wrong that we (the Western World) have so much more than those in other parts of the world. Although this is a kind intention, she's trying to force her will on others.

If you genuinely want to make a difference to someone else's life - put the thought into the Universe. A person or organisation who would like your help will then be brought to you. Ask them what they want, and tailor your offering accordingly.

The Law of Attraction is incredibly powerful. Who knows what wonderful things the Universe will manifest for all of us if we send out thoughts for ourselves and others!

Quote: *"**How wonderful it is that nobody need wait a single moment before starting to improve the world**"* - Anne Frank

15. Conflicting Intentions and the Law of Attraction

Each of us ultimately controls of what the Law of Attraction brings to us. We can only influence what others attract if their subconscious gives this permission. Sometimes we're influenced by other, stronger, energies but this is because we've given permission for this to happen.

Of course conflict does exist, but this is external conflict where two opposing energies declare their intention. These opposing energies create the conflict situation.

However, most of the conflict we perceive is internal to us. Others don't see or feel the conflict; it's simply our mind creating conflicting thoughts. This type of conflict is a waste of energy.

To clarify my point about internal conflict: Imagine you and a colleague apply for the same promotion at work. Only one can be successful as there's only one position available. Your subconscious mind likes competition so you create an internal conflict.

Now you've decided there is a conflict you probably have an internal dialogue about who will get the job. You may even be deciding how this promotion is going to affect your professional relationship.

At worst, your inner voice might start telling you that you won't get the job. If this is your belief then really it's a waste of time going to the interview. Your inner voice is already telling the Universe that you don't want the job.

You have no idea how much this promotion really matters to your colleague. You don't know whether he/she is having positive or negative thoughts about the outcome. This conflict is internal to you. The best advice is decide how important the promotion is to you. If you really want it focus on getting it and send that vibration to the Universe.

Quote: ***"No man is defeated without until he has first be defeated within"*** - Eleanor Roosevelt

Here's another example of internal conflict for you to consider. You want your special relationship to be better, but your spouse doesn't appear to want the same thing.

What's happening here is you're projecting an intention for yourself and a conflicting one for your spouse. Without any evidence you've created an internal conflict and turned it into your reality.

How do you know that your spouse perceives your relationship to be a problem? He/she may be happy with things as they are, and may feel there is nothing to fix. Who's right and who's wrong in this situation?

Reflection: Conflict situation

1. Spend a little time on your internal conflict experiences. You may have a similar experience to the ones mentioned here, or something completely different

2. What made you create this internal conflict? Did you stop it before it became an external conflict?

3. What did you learn from the experience; if anything?

4. Have you continued to create internal conflict situations, or have you learnt your lesson?

If you encourage this internal conflict you will eventually create an external conflict situation that you both experience. In truth, you can only fix a problem if both energies perceive there is a problem and you both want to fix the situation.

My question to you is -"why create conflict situations in the first place?" We all feel better and happier when we don't have conflict in our lives. Food for thought?

Quote: ***"The Universe never asked you to struggle. It is simply answering your mood"***
- Abraham Hicks

16. Our Reality and the Law of Attraction

Modern society is constantly looking for proof, but the Law of Attraction isn't always tangible. We can't smell it, touch it or hear it, but the Law of Attraction is real.

As it's intangible many dismiss the Law of Attraction as spiritual mumbo jumbo. Even believers have moments of doubt. Although this is normal it might be helpful to revisit your reflection from chapter 6.

The changes created by the Law of Attraction can't always be seen by the naked eye. The proof of the Law of Attraction is how each of us feels. Whether we're seeking material goods or emotional experiences, our prime motivation is happiness.

Happiness is internal, which is why we all create our own reality. No matter who meet, what we have or what we experience we choose how we feel about it. We choose whether to be happy or not; we choose whether it's a good experience for us or not.

Let's say you want a brand-new Porsche. This is a totally achievable goal, and so you set to work on manifesting it. Eventually you get your new Porsche. You've attracted exactly what you said you wanted, but only you know if this makes you happy of not.

The Law of Attraction is about swapping negative thoughts for positive ones. It's all about focusing on what you want more of, instead of what you want less of.

Our intention (vibration) creates our reality. Or, to put it another way - we are our intentions. Confused? Here's my take on it:

1. Consciously or unconsciously we all make choices about all aspects of our lives

2. These choices shape our vision, beliefs, values, habits and actions

3. This is the Law of Nature. Like it or not, we are all subject to nature's laws

4. If our intention is strong enough we will create a vibration, which the Law of Attraction acts on

5. There are two kinds of intentions - conscious and unconscious. Hence, our ability to attract the things we don't actually want

6. What we manifest is the result of the Law of Attraction and the Law of Manifestation working

7. Our reality is partly the physical outcome (e.g. the Porsche on the driveway) and partly our emotional response i.e. happiness or dissatisfaction with the outcome

Reflection: My reality

1. Spend a little time reflecting on something that you really wanted, and successfully manifested

2. Were you pleased or dissatisfied with the outcome? Did you feel exactly how you expected to feel?

3. Were you so busy focusing on achieving your goal that you forgot to imagine how it would feel to manifest your desire?

The reality of our life currently is the result of the thoughts (vibrations) we put into the Universe in the past. Some of these vibrations may have been generated before we were born. For whatever reason we have chosen our life experiences, and this is what we are manifesting now.

We could all go to the same seminar, get the same advice and be given the same opportunities. For each of us the outcome would be different as we would all create a different vibration. Each of us would have a different perception of the reality created. Some of us would feel happy and contented but others would feel dissatisfied.

We all create our own reality. No one else can do this for us as we're the controller of our thoughts. Never again underestimate the power of thought. The power of thought attracts what we focus on, but the 'reality' is our perception of the outcome. No one can share your reality.

Quote: ***"Man, alone, has the power to transform his thoughts into physical reality; man, alone, can dream and make his dreams come true"*** - Napoleon Hill

17. The Top 10 Law of Attraction Mistakes

From time to time we all make mistakes when using the Law of Attraction. I thought it might be helpful to explain the top 10 Law of Attraction mistakes. If we know where we're going wrong we can consciously do something about it.

1. Unclear intentions

If we aren't very clear about what we want it's unrealistic to expect the Universe to deliver it. Imagine going to the train station and buying a ticket to 'anywhere'. We can't blame the rail company when we end up in a place we don't want to be.

We all think we know what we want, but in reality we have a much clearer idea of what we don't want. If we want the Law of Attraction to give us all the material goods, experiences and sense of wellbeing that we desire, we must be clear about what we **do** want.

Create the right vibration and expect to get the right results.

2. Beliefs

Even if we can clearly state what we truly want, that isn't the whole process. Belief is the most important element. We have to believe 100% that we will attract our desired outcome when the time is right.

Overcoming our self-limiting beliefs is the hardest part of successfully harnessing the Law of Attraction. What we state needs to be aligned to our deep-rooted beliefs i.e. we are worthy of the best the Universe has to offer. Without belief we're doomed to failure; or at least limited success.

3. Our intentions are a secret

Of course we don't want to tell everyone about our heart's desires, but most manifestations require input from other energies. It's important to decide who we trust to share our thoughts and intentions with.

As I've said previously, we have to give the Universe a helping hand. We also need to be receptive when opportunities present themselves. Sometimes others will make opportunities available to us if they know what we want.

4. We become a victim

We fall into the trap of saying things like "when I have the money, when I find that special person or my dream job etc". This immediately creates a vibration of 'lack and scarcity'.

The Universe responds to the strongest vibration. In this case the desire is I want the things I don't currently have. The stronger vibration is therefore scarcity. The Universe then delivers more of the same as it's simply responding to our strongest vibration.

One of my clients is constantly job hunting. Each time she's near the top of the list of preferred candidates, but never quite secures the job. Why? Her rider to each application she fills in is "I don't expect to get it, but I hope I do". Enough said!

5. We try to dictate how

Some of us are incapable of simply asking, believing and receiving. As a natural control freak, I've been guilty of this in the past. It's taken lots of practice to break this habit.

Instead of trusting the Universe to do its job, we have to try to get involved in the 'how'. No matter how well intentioned, this interference gets in the way of allowing the Universe to do its job.

It may be difficult, learn to relax and trust the Universe to manifest what you desire when the time is right. Of course we have to be open to spotting opportunities and receiving but we don't have to provide the Universe with detailed instructions. The Universe knows how to do its job!

6. We pass judgement too soon

Some of us give up and declare failure too soon. We decide we want something in a very specific (and usually very short) timescale, and when this doesn't happen we judge the Law of Attraction to have failed us.

This is a big mistake. The Universe will always deliver what we ask for, or something better, when the time is right. This may not always be the timescale that we set for ourselves.

By nature I'm impatient and spent much of my childhood being told "I hope you get what you want while you still want it". Over time, I've learnt to trust the Universe to deliver what I want, at the right time. If I no longer want something, I simply change the vibration.

7. Gratitude

Gratitude is massively important when working with the Law of Attraction. Sometimes we disregard a manifestation simply because it didn't happen in the way we had decided it should.

Perhaps you asked for £100,000 by the end of the year. You then received a letter offering you a loan for £100,000. You dismiss this as it's not what you asked for; when actually the Universe is giving you the means to have £100,000 to spend. The Universe can't be blamed if you didn't say how you wanted to get this money.

Be grateful for everything the Universe gives you. The more grateful you are the more the Universe will give you.

8. Change of routine

Sometimes we want something and we want it now. As we're so convinced that it's going to happen we start living our dream life immediately. By all means start to make small changes in your lifestyle but don't take it to the extreme.

Perhaps you've decided that you want a new car. Don't go into debt to buy the car just because you know you will eventually be able to afford it. Your ego will go into survival mode. This immediately creates vibrational conflict and plays havoc with the Law of Attraction.

9. Too self-centred

Sometimes we don't stop at just focusing on what we want. We may focus on what we want and simultaneously create a vibration that doesn't want others to manifest their heart's desires too. Although not very nice, this is a common human trait.

Being totally self-centred and not wishing good things for others creates an energy blockage. Energy blockages prevent the Law of Attraction from manifesting for the benefit of everyone. There's plenty for everyone so why not wish everyone the best the Universe can offer.

10. Outcome obsessed

Sometimes we become so obsessed with believing that we create a vibration that suggests desperation. This desperation suggests scarcity, and so we simply attract more of the same.

There's a fine line between believing and obsessing. It's important to believe, but also relax and trust the Universe to deliver what we want. Relaxed believing is quite different to desperation.

Quote: ***"I attract into my life whatever I give my attention, energy and focus to, whether postive or negative"*** - Michael Losier

18. Conclusion

Are you still convinced that the Law of Attraction doesn't work? Are you a person who is driven by logic? If so, it's important to understand that not everything in life can be defined by logic. Sometimes the logical decision doesn't lead to the greatest happiness.

If you believe in the Law of Gravity why is it so difficult to believe in the Law of Attraction?

Perhaps you're one of those people who say "if it's so easy why don't more people do it?" Good question. I believe there are three common reasons why people don't consciously practice the Law of Attraction. These are:

1. They don't know about the Law of Attraction

2. They've heard about it, but don't believe in it enough to make it work

3. Some people are naturally cynical and convince themselves it's nothing more than new age mumbo jumbo

These people are potentially missing out on so much, but that's their choice, as we all have free will.

The Law of Attraction can be our friend or foe. If we choose to make the Law of Attraction our friend then we're the lucky ones who benefit from it greatly.

There's a common misconception that those who believe in the Law of Attraction are very materialistic. Most of us who choose to consciously harness the Law of Attraction don't simply fill our lives with material goods. Instead we have a balance of material goods, experiences and a sense of wellbeing.

To finish, here's a real success story that can easily be verified. Julie Andrews overcame early childhood extreme poverty. Added to this her parents divorced, and World War II broke out.

Against all the odds she stayed focused on positive thoughts (consciously or unconsciously). By the age of 10, Julie was able to start her stage career. Since then she has gone on to enjoy huge success and become a multi-award winning star.

We won't all manifest such phenomenal success but we can all choose a positive path. The choice really is ours.

If you're still struggling to believe in the success of the Law of Attraction, look for examples of success stories. There are plenty of success stories to choose from. You'll find this information readily available in books, DVDs, online video clips and the internet; to name just a few options.

I wish you every success harnessing the power of the Law of Attraction.

Quote: ***"As soon as you start to feel differently about what you already have, you will start to attract more of the good things, more of the things you can be grateful for"*** - Joe Vitale

www.ingramcontent.com/pod-product-compliance
Ingram Content Group UK Ltd.
Pitfield, Milton Keynes, MK11 3LW, UK
UKHW020220250726
13967UKWH00001B/95

9 780992 947903